SAVED BY SAGO: A PASTOR'S PERSPECTIVE

BY
REV. ANDREW KRANYC

McClain Printing Company
Parsons, WV 26287
2006

International Standard Book Number 0-87012-749-7
Printed in the United States of America
Copyright © 2006 by Fr. Andrew Kranyc
Philippi, WV
All Rights Reserved
2006

Reprinted 2006

McClain Printing Company
Parsons, West Virginia
www.mcclainprinting.com
2006

Photo credits

Front cover: Sago Baptist Church
Back cover: Sago Mine Cleaning Plant

*Photos courtesy of: Sam Santilli Photography
Philippi, West Virginia
304-457-4217*

*A Special Thank You to
Michelle Mullenax-McKinnie
Vice President of Publishing
McClain Printing Company
for all her
graciousness and help in
publishing this book.*

DEDICATED TO

MY FATHER, ANDY KRANYC, SR.
(a retired coal miner)
AND TO MY MOTHER, GILDA,
AND MY SISTER, CYNTHIA,
BOTH OF WHOM ARE COAL MINERS' DAUGHTERS

IN MEMORY OF

THOMAS ANDERSON
GEORGE JUNIOR HAMNER
ALVA MARTIN BENNETT
JIM BENNETT
JERRY GROVES
TERRY HELMS
JESSE JONES
DAVID LEWIS
MARTIN TOLER
FRED WARE, JR.
JACK WEAVER
MARSHALL WINANS

AND WITH CONTINUED PRAYERS FOR
RANDAL McCLOY, JR.

FOREWORD

This book concerning the events of the Sago mine disaster will hold you "spell-bound" and you will not be able to put it down until every page is read. You will laugh, cry, and experience many emotions as you read this book.

I first met Fr. Andy at the Sago Baptist Church on the first day of the disaster and immediately felt a kindred spirit as though I had known him all my life. He is a warm, compassionate human being. He is a true "ambassador of Jesus Christ."

This experience has truly humbled us all and has brought us together as "one" as Jesus prayed in His intercessory prayer to the Father in St. John's gospel, chapter 17. This was a life changing experience for all of us and will deeply affect your life also as the events of those few days unfold in the pages of this book.

After reading the book, I would encourage you to call upon the Lord and pray in your own way. Acknowledge the fact that "all have sinned" and ask Jesus Christ to save you and come into your heart. Our prayers are with the families and we will meet these miners and our loved ones in heaven one day soon. What a reunion that will be!

Rev. Randy Hughes, D.Min.
Senior Pastor
Weston Church of God

INTRODUCTION

I am not a native West Virginian. I was born and raised in the little coal town of Windber, PA which is only a few miles from Johnstown, PA and likewise from both the Quecreek Mine Disaster and Flight 93. "Windber" was named after the Berwind Coal Co. which operated all the mines around our town. To this very day, sections of our town are referred to as Mine 32, Mine 35, Mine 36, Mine 37, Mine 40, and Mine 42. Our local church cemetery is located in the area of Mine 34, and all of the old-timers, in referring to death, would say that one day we would all be together "in 34." Through the years, over 400 miners lost their lives in the coal mines around Windber.

My father, both grandfathers, and most of my uncles were all coal miners. Growing up, I assumed I would become a miner as well. However, my father refused to permit me to go into the mines. He said, "The way you are with tools, you would be dead within two weeks." So I became a teacher and eventually a priest.

I first came to West Virginia in 1987 as a Franciscan stationed at Our Lady of Perpetual Help Church in Stonewood. After leaving the Franciscans and working as an In-Home Family Preservation Therapist with Appalachian Mental Health and Try-Again Homes, I became a priest of the Diocese of Wheeling-Charleston, which includes our entire state. For many years I served as Pastor of Sacred Heart and St. Peter Claver Parishes in Huntington, as well as Catholic Chaplain at the V.A. Medical Center. After being on medical leave for heart surgery, I am currently assigned as Pastor of St. Elizabeth Parish in Philippi and Catholic Chaplain at Alderson-Broaddus College.

As soon as I open my mouth, everyone knows that I am a "foreigner." Yet I have served my entire priesthood here in West Virginia. I fell in love with this state and its people and have spent the past 19 years as an "adopted" Mountaineer. I even cheer for WVU when they play Pitt!

To me, the miners and families of Sago exemplify all that is best about this state and this little book of reflections is both a tribute to them and, for me, a thank you to all the West Virginians who have made me feel at home here all these years. This little book began as a personal journal, but it was suggested to me that perhaps if made into a book it could be of help in raising additional monies for the miners' families and coal miners in general. A percentage of the profits from this book will go directly to the Sago miner families. I hope that I have accurately and fittingly expressed the spirit and courage of the people, and if there are places in which I have failed in this, it is because I am still a West Virginian "in progress."

Our little town of Philippi is famous for its covered bridge…the longest one in the United States. A covered bridge provides shelter for those making a crossing in life. It is my hope that this little book will be a "covered bridge" to help all those touched by Sago as they travel through this transitional time in their lives, and cross from the sadness of the death of a loved one to new life.

I would encourage you to read this book only one chapter at a time and to reflect a bit on each section, perhaps reading a passage of Scripture and saying a little prayer for the miners and their families as you do so. May God bless and keep you and all coal miners and their families everywhere.

TABLE OF CONTENTS

Chapter 1:	O Holiday Tree, O Holiday Tree	1
Chapter 2:	Almost Heaven	5
Chapter 3:	Coal Miners' Daughters	9
Chapter 4:	Someone You Can Count On	11
Chapter 5:	Myth Conceptions	15
Chapter 6:	We Are Family	19
Chapter 7:	The Coat of Many Colors	23
Chapter 8:	Between a Rock and a Heart Place	27
Chapter 9:	Feathers in the Wind	31
Chapter 10:	The Beast	35
Chapter 11:	Scars Into Stars	39
Chapter 12:	The Hatfields and the McCloys	43
Chapter 13:	State of the Union	49
Chapter 14:	We're Not in Kansas Anymore, Toto	53
Chapter 15:	Sweet Home Alabama	57
Chapter 16:	Saved by Sago	61

Chapter 1:
O Holiday Tree, O Holiday Tree

Barely a week before the events that unfolded at the Sago mine, many Americans were angered and saddened at the latest annual attempt to "take Christ out of Christmas." To wish someone a Merry "Christmas" was now politically incorrect. There was to be no such thing as a "Christmas" tree. The preferred language was to be "Happy Holidays" or "Season's Greetings" as we gathered around our "Holiday" tree. The 60's assertion that "God is Dead" was no longer even relevant, for God was now to be ignored whether dead or alive as America continued its decades-long slide into a totally generic brand X culture. Most people who travel about this great nation are noticing more and more the demise of regionalism, as Elmer's Country Store and Auntie Mae's Biscuits gradually give way to the same old, same old suburbia department stores and fast food chains. The same thing is happening in our minds and hearts as we create a spiritual suburbia of similar generic blandness. Taking "Christ" out of "Christmas" is like taking the Varsity hot dog shop out of Atlanta, only with a lot more serious consequences.

Then out of nowhere, from deep within the Appalachian backbone of this country, came a group of miners who single-handedly put God-questions, prayer, and discussions of faith right smack-dab back into the center of our attention. Is it all just a tragic coincidence, or are the Sago miners a catalyst for a spiritual renewal in this land of ours? Were their lives simply a matter of "dust to coal dust?" Or did their sacrifice serve to highlight important faith lessons we badly need to recover and understand? How is it that a culture that insists on brand name clothing, electronics, and cars settles so easily and unthinkingly on a brand X spirituality? Is the tragedy of Sago that 12 good men lost their lives because of a freak of nature or human incompetence? Or does the sacrifice of Sago remind us that there is no greater tragedy than the culture of meaninglessness?

There are serious reasons why we need to keep Christ in Christmas. Without that, the human story makes no sense and leaves us with a dismal end to contemplate. Proponents of Brand X will never win, because in the end, Christmas offers a better story than they do.

We Christians believe that Christmas is the eye of the storm. Anyone who has been in a hurricane knows the screaming winds, the crashing trees, the torrential downpour, the crackling of downed power lines. Then, all of a sudden, comes the eye of the storm when everything becomes still. Not a leaf quivers…not a sound is heard. And then, once more, the buffeting winds and stinging rains and flying branches. But that experience of the eye of the storm…the still point…is one that is never forgotten.

Christmas is like that. It comes in the middle of the storm of biblical history. From the great flood of Noah to Hebrew slavery in Egypt, from the Babylonian Captivity to the occupation by the Romans, from the Black Death to nuclear war, the Word of God became Incarnate right in the middle of it all to provide humanity with a still point, a moment's peace, in the midst of the storms of life and history.

If those who would like to take Christ out of Christmas have their way, our nation will be buffeted by the storms of history without any place of safety or refuge. The Sago miners have helped to restore a faith sensibility…they have helped put Christ back into the forefront of the debate on the future of our society and culture. At Christmas time, good little boys and girls who have been naughty are told that they will get a lump of coal in their stockings instead of gifts. Maybe the Sago miners gave us a lump of coal in our "happy holiday" stockings this year to remind us to put Christ back into Christmas.

Chapter 2: Almost Heaven

Someone once said that West Virginia is the most northern of southern states, the most southern of northern states, the most eastern of western states, and the most western of eastern states. The lyrics of John Denver call us to these country roads that take us home…not only to the homes in the hills and hollers of the Mountain State, but HOME for all Americans.

West Virginia is the last great American reservation. The final refuge. Here we are, surrounded by Columbus, Cleveland, Pittsburgh, Philadelphia, New York, Baltimore, Washington D.C., Richmond, Charlotte, and Cincinnati. Right in the middle of the greatest population centers in the eastern U.S. is this breathtaking land of mountains and streams, hills and lakes. A place where whitetail deer outnumber people. Sago is right on the Buckhannon River, a famous fishing stream with hundreds of fishing camps that draw visitors every summer from all over our nation. Upshur and Barbour counties in West Virginia are places where the aforementioned "city folk" come to "get away from it all." This is a place where a person can break free of the rat race for awhile and truly feel "almost in heaven." Parts of the Buckhannon River near Sago have solid rock beds and the water is so crystal clear that you can see the bottom of the river. It's people are like that too: solid in their faith, with a clear value system.

West Virginia is truly America's "Mountain Mama." Many of the "old" values the rest of America has lost are still strong here. Homer Hickam, one of West Virginia's most well-known sons on whose life the movie "October Sky" was based, wrote a book about WV coal miners ("We Are Not Afraid") in which he insightfully delineates the main values of the coal culture of these hills. He shows that the four pillars of our coal miner culture are: 1) being proud of who we are; 2) standing up for what we believe in; 3) keeping our families together; and 4) trusting in God but relying on ourselves.

So many Americans today are not proud of the work they do, feeling like insignificant drones in some corporate beehive. Wanting Christ out of Christmas is symptomatic of a wider disinclination to profess beliefs in general. Too many of us have become wishy-washy, wet noodle, spineless creatures with nothing in particular to live for, let alone die for. American families today are scattered far and wide around the country. Families turn their heads away from elderly loved ones and prefer to let social service agencies provide the care that family members are too selfish or too distant to provide themselves. The American family has disintegrated almost beyond recognition. As for trust in God, how can we trust God when most of us don't even trust ourselves anymore? We don't trust our government. We don't trust our priests. We don't trust our schools. We don't trust anything or anyone. It is no wonder so many no longer believe in God. How can we believe in God when we don't believe in ourselves?

There can scarcely be a state of the union that has been more exploited throughout its history than West Virginia. Not only were the coal, lumber and gas industries mostly controlled by out-of-state owners, but even the local native Americans were subject to larger and more powerful out-of-state tribes. Even the creation of our state was due to a desire to be independent from the control of a more populous and powerful eastern Virginia. Any American who feels exploited by their employer shares a kinship with us here. This land knows how unfair life can be.

Yet although many have come here to ravish our land, take our resources, and laugh and make fun of our customs,

West Virginians stand tall and proud about who they are and their way of life. We don't blame God for the unfairness of life. We are much too close to His creation on a daily basis to do that. We don't tell other people how to live their lives. But here, we remember what our daddies and our granddaddies and our great granddaddies taught us and we keep those values alive and strong. Just as General Thomas Jackson, a native of West Virginia, stood like a stone wall at the Battle of Manassas, the people of this state stand like a stone wall against the encroachment of suburbanization, commercialization, and secularization into these hills. We are the Rock of Refuge in the middle of that ring of cities, holding on to God, Country, and Family. Come here, and you will recapture the foundations this nation was built on. There is an old joke that talking to God is easier here because it is a "local call"…for "Almost Heaven" is not just this state, but the state of mind that exists here.

Note: The references to Homer Hickam are from his book "We Are Not Afraid," which is available from the publisher, Health Communications, Inc. 3201 S.W. 15th St., Deerfield Beach, Fl 33442-8190. Also recommended for an understanding of the coal culture of WV are his books: "The Coalwood Way" and "Sky of Stone."

Chapter 3:
Coal Miners' Daughters

As the news media covered the story of Sago, many around the nation were incredulous as to how anyone could possibly work in the coal mines for a living. What would drive someone into such a dangerous job? Why would anyone choose mining as their occupation?

Here in this state, coal mining is not an occupation. It is a way of life. It is the predominant way of life and the predominant culture of our state. Many of the Sago miners came from families that have been mining coal for 150 years. There are few other options in the area for jobs that pay as well. But it isn't just the money. Coal miners are proud of what they do. They see their jobs as patriotic. They are providing the energy on which America operates. Every single person in this country benefits from coal. From every time a light switch is flipped on to every time a foot is set on a subway, our daily conveniences and conveyances operate on energy from coal production.

Nearly every family in this state is either involved in coal mining or has relatives and friends who are. It is said that there is enough coal under West Virginia to provide America with energy for the next 300 years. If West Virginia is our "Mountain Mama," then its women are coal miners' daughters. Many of the women here are coal miners themselves. These countless "loretta lynns" are the backbone of the entire value system. They are the Rachels and Ruths who pray unceasingly to God for the safety of their husbands, sons, and brothers down in those mines. They are the ones who put the little added touches in the miners' lunch buckets: the special home made cookies as a reminder of what he is risking his life for; the tiny little bite out of his sandwich to remind him his lunch was packed with love; the little crayon drawings of his grandchild added into the bucket. They send their men off into the mines the way other wives send their men off to war…knowing that it may be the last moment to see them alive. No one on earth can pray like a coal miner's wife or daughter or mother. They were the ones huddled together at Sago Baptist Church, storming heaven on behalf of their loved ones. No more fervent and sincere praying has ever been heard upon this continent.

Their prayers had a mother's touch to them. The main scripture passages read and prayed about at Sago were ones about shepherding lambs, sheltering under a mother's wings, words becoming flesh, and bringing good from bad. All of these are MOTHERS' prayers! Who can understand the beginning of John's Gospel better than an expectant mother? Who understands Paul's assurance that all things work together for good for those who love God more than mothers, who know how to kiss a child's boo-boos and make them better? The spirit and prayers of Sago cannot be understood unless one understands them as the prayers of coal miners' daughters, mothers, and wives. They are prayers about giving birth, nourishing and growing new life, and tending to life's hurts. When people who understand those things pray that way, no matter what the final outcome of the specific event, those prayers WILL grow new life and WILL work together to nourish something good from the ashes of the coal buckets. You can join them in their prayers. The next time you step onto a subway in one of our major cities, remember to say a little prayer for the coal miner whose blood, sweat and tears made the electricity for your ride downtown possible.

Chapter 4:
Someone You Can Count On

In many of the interviews during the aftermath of Sago, people were asked if belief in God...if a personal faith life...was important to coal miners. It has been said that there are no atheists in foxholes or coal mines. Most coal miners are not overly ostentatious about their spirituality. They go to work. They go to church. They work hard and pray hard. They don't get very emotional and don't show off. But it is the basis of their lives. Go to any coal mining town in any part of this country and you will be guaranteed to find several churches there dating back to the beginnings of that community.

The reason so many today do not understand miners or their faith is because we have become a nation puffed up with pride. We exalt ourselves every chance we get: from the celebrations after scoring touchdowns to the designer labels on our clothing. We have lost our sense of humility. Think about foxholes and coal mines. Both of them require a "lowering." A digging "down." A "stooping over." A posture of humility. Jesus said that those who exalted themselves would be humbled and those who humbled themselves would be exalted. Coal miners work in an environment where very often heads must be bowed to avoid hitting the low ceilings of the coal seams. In such a state of constant humility, one quickly is cognizant of a "greater power."

The miners at Sago were men of great faith. All of them. The crew that perished in that mine gathered together and prayed before every single shift…before setting one foot into that mine. One of the miners, as he rode into the mine, daily took his finger and scrawled in the coal dust on the mantrip car the words "Jesus Saves." Another of the miners ended the message on his telephone answering machine with the words: "Do you know the Lord as your Savior?" One of the men had recently been baptized. One had been praying for many years for his father to be saved. That father accepted Jesus as his Lord and Savior at Sago Baptist Church the night the announcements were made. Another of the miners taught Sunday school weekly to the young adults of his church. He also filled in when the minister had to be away and was known as a great preacher in his own right.

Not only is one's personal faith important to a coal miner, but so is the status of his coworker's faith life. Coal miners know well the inherent dangers of their job. They want to know when the chips are down that they can count on the people they work with to be there for them. If someone truly believes in God, whether Christian, Jewish, Muslim or Buddhist, we like to think that person will tend to be a little less selfish and a little more concerned about his fellow human beings than someone who does not believe in God. There are those who will be quick to point out the wars in the name of religion throughout history and the current situation with terrorism in the Middle East as examples of faithful people treating fellow human beings poorly. However, I would submit that those past wars and current terrorist activities have much more to do with politics than with religion. I would also point out that I am talking about FAITH, not religion…there often being a great difference between the two.

When Jesus died on the cross, all of his disciples ran and abandoned him except for John. They had not yet received the faith of the resurrection. At Sago, all the miners stuck together and tried to help one another in the moment of death. They had resurrection faith! Think of the people in your life that you can REALLY count on when the chips are down. How many of them are atheists?

Chapter 5: Myth Conceptions

Any time there is a tragedy, be it the Johnstown Flood, 911, Hurricane Katrina, or the Sago mine disaster, there are always those who will blame it on a vengeful God who cares little for his human subjects and takes great pleasure in tormenting them with all manner of tsunamis, earthquakes, pestilences, and violence. For many people, God is like the bully we all knew as children who liked to pull the legs and wings off grasshoppers and butterflies. As speculation of the cause of the Sago explosion included the possibility of a lightning strike due to the severe storm in the area that morning, it was but a small step for many to blame God as the divine archer of that thunderbolt.

This is NOT the kind of God that Christians believe in. The god of lightning and thunder, if anything, is Zeus of Greek mythology…a religious system that quickly gave way when confronted by the new teachings of Christianity. Why is it that so many people today continue to hold on to the debris and flotsam of dead religions, preferring that to the living God?

One reason many point fingers at God in this manner is because of the desire for pride and power our society has today. We see personal POWER programs everywhere. So many TV series and movies today are about magical ways of having POWER over others. A misreading of the Hebrew Scriptures often feeds into this. As one reads the mighty acts of God in Genesis, Exodus, Daniel and other books of Scripture, we become caught up in God's POWER. The result of this is that we tend to think of "miracles" as God's use of power in a flashy, sensational manner.

In the New Testament however, Jesus more often that not exercises his divine abilities not through mighty acts of power but in times of illness and weakness and death. Jesus heals those who are crippled, those who are hemorrhaging, those who have leprosy. He feeds the hungry. God's "power" is revealed in times of weakness more so than in times of strength. Before his Passion, when his disciples and friends wanted to whisk him away from danger, Jesus told them that he could have legions of angels at his command if he so desired. But he was going to reveal his power to us through suffering and weakness and death instead. Therefore, when we Christians look to find the presence of God in the events of our lives, we need to look in the weak and broken places. In regard to Sago, this means that it does us a disservice to look for God in the lightning and the destruction. If God was to be found anywhere at Sago, he was gasping for breath with the miners and embracing the weeping women in the church. Christ brings new life out of death and goodness out of horror.

Everyone prayed that the Sago miners be saved…that the miners be rescued. But God ended up having the Sago miners save us! It is the miners who have rescued us! All the ministers in the area can attest to the fact that in the days during and after Sago, many people came to Sunday services that had not been to church in years…maybe never. Hundreds of people accepted Christ as their Lord and Savior and were saved…many right at Sago Baptist Church during the ordeal itself. Many young people have decided to become ministers and give their lives to the service of God because of what happened here. Family members who hadn't talked with one another in years came back together at Sago. Estranged husbands and wives found their relationships rekindled. Teens who thought their parents were "out of it" suddenly were filled with pride. God heard the prayers of the people for rescue and salvation. But instead of rescuing 12 men, he decided to use them to rescue 1200 or 12,000 others. After all, in our short-sightedness, did we really think that the Sago miners were the only ones trapped in a confined space? Aren't millions of Americans trapped in small confined hearts and souls? Or trapped in situations they can't get out of? Aren't millions of Americans struggling for a breath of fresh air? Hasn't life exploded in the faces of many Americans? Oh yes, the prayers of those coal miners' daughters WERE heard…not for their men…but for YOU!

Chapter 6: We Are Family

Upon arriving at Sago Baptist Church the first day of the ordeal, one became part of a crowd of people of all ages, races and creeds. It was a conglomeration of teary-eyed concerned people who in one way or another were connected with the 13 men down in that mine. TV was not enough, you see. You had to BE there. You had to be close to the person you loved who was down in that hole.

It didn't take long for that mishmash of people to become family. 13 families quickly became one family. Family is a major concept in West Virginia. As Homer Hickam states, keeping our families together is one of the major priorities here. When you meet a West Virginian for the first time, he or she is much more likely to ask you who you are related to than what you do for a living. Knowing one's family background is an essential part of the culture here.

Much of this is rooted in the Christian tradition. Matthew begins his gospel with the genealogy of Jesus…with Abraham begetting Isaac and Isaac begetting Jacob and so on. Jesus then calls Peter, Andrew and Paul. Paul calls Timothy. Timothy called someone else. And if you are a Christian someone called you. This living tradition is part and parcel of the notion of family that exists in West Virginia and among the people who were at Sago. We were family in that we were from the hills of West Virginia. We were family in that we shared the bond of coal mining. We were family in that we were part of the long line of those called in the Christian tradition. All the ingredients existed for an instant bonding. Now that the miners have all had their funerals and the media has left the area, many people present at the Sago ordeal feel almost saddened to be apart from each other. The bonds formed there in those three days will last forever. So many new friendships were formed.

This was accomplished through food and fellowship, music, and prayer. When entering the side door of Sago Baptist Church, one steps into the hall, which in those days had tables laden with food and families huddling around coffee and a sandwich...telling stories about their loved one trapped in the mine and getting to know the other families. Some of the trapped miners' families already knew each other. One notices in the gospels how many times Jesus used food and meals to bring people together.

Pastor Jerry Murrell of the Way of Holiness Church was present throughout the ordeal at Sago and regularly offered his gift of music in the chapel, soothing strained nerves and helping the distraught to reflect upon their lives. At several crucial moments during the two days, his music calmed frayed nerves and many people would come and sit in the pews with their arms around one another's shoulders, or holding hands, and often quietly or even silently mouthing the words to the tune being played.

At one point during the second night, before any announcement had been made, an impromptu prayer service materialized almost spontaneously from the hearts of everyone in that little church. Revs. Wease Day and Ed McDaniels helped to lead the most fervent moment of prayer I have ever witnessed in my life. Everyone stood and joined hands to sing "Amazing Grace," and that tune has NEVER in its entire history been sung with such sincerity and emotion. I will never hear it again without thinking of Sago. At the final verse everyone raised their hands in the air and sang "Praise God" and every soul was lifted up to God.

During that service we prayed not only that the miners be rescued, but we prayed strongly and often that whatever God's will turned out to be, that we would be able to accept it in faith. And that prayer was answered. In the early morning hours after the bad news stunned us all, the news media enjoyed highlighting those who shouted blasphemies to God and threats to company and government officials. Interestingly enough, the media did not show that only a short hour later, those same individuals, who had suffered a very understandable emotional and spiritual breakdown, returned to apologize to everyone they had shouted at, including God. You see, that's how a FAMILY is. People say what they think and let their emotions and frustrations and anger out, but in the end we still love one another. That is what the media couldn't understand. The coal miner families of West Virginia speak what is on their minds and hearts but in the end they are sealed as a family and those seals never burst the way the ones in the Sago mine did. We might get angry and frustrated at times with one another and we might very well say those things to one another…but we are family. No outsider better talk that way to us. But within our family, we know that we can share our deepest feelings and still be accepted and loved in the end. What happened at Sago after the stunning bad news arrived was NOT a loss of faith…it was a celebration of what FAMILY is all about…and no place does it any better than West Virginia.

Chapter 7:
The Coat of Many Colors

The musical "Joseph's Amazing Technicolor Dreamcoat" has given enjoyment to many people, but I have never seen a more beautiful "coat of many colors" than that in the Sago Baptist Church. During the ordeal at Sago, I was the only Catholic priest present, but at no time during those days were there ever fewer than 15 ministers of every denomination present for the families…Methodist, Baptist, Catholic, Presbyterian, Pentecostal, Episcopal…the list could go on and on.

If one were to have been present with those ministers at Sago, one would never have imagined that there could ever have been a history of schism between the Christian denominations for so many centuries. Every minister present cooperated fully with the others, and the members of the miners' families freely availed themselves of whatever minister was available regardless of denomination. Baptists talked to Catholic priests and Methodists talked with Church of God ministers. There were male ministers and female ministers present at all times. Several were married couples who were both ordained clergy. Some were new ministers and some were retired ones who had served their churches for decades. They prayed not only with the family members but with and for each other. They fed off of each other's strength and cried with each other in their weakness. Without the tremendous ministerial bonds that happened almost instantly at Sago, no minister could have withstood the emotional rollercoaster of those days. How could one minister to grieving families when feeling shattered in one's own heart? The only way was to share one's brokenness with a fellow minister who understood. For me personally, those persons were Rev. Randy Hughes of the Church of God, and Rev. Mitch Griffin (a retired Methodist minister). If only the leaders of our churches could do the same and end this scandalous, scandalous division that has gone on way too long in Christianity. The world needs fewer theologians at the pulpit and more arthritic broken down old warriors for Christ who are willing to get their shoes ruined in the mud of Sago, and who may have lost their youth but not their hearts.

To all the young people who have been moved by Sago into considering a vocation as a priest or minister in their respective congregations, I assure you that all of us in Christ's service at Sago are praying for you to persevere, for God is certainly calling you forth for a purpose. Serving God is not about academic theological debate. It's about tears and mud and blood in places like Sago which exist in the hearts of millions of Americans. It's been said that the biggest problem with church leadership today is antibiotics, for they have kept antiquated minds alive to preserve antiquated ideas. The world also needs the fervor and energy of young people willing to rub shoulders with whoever has showed up, in order to get the job done.

The ministers at Sago took the coat of many colors, which Joseph's brothers (i.e. the leaders of the world's denominations) tore apart and bloodied, and transformed it into the seamless cloak of Jesus Christ at Calvary. How many colors are you willing to include in the coat of your heart and soul?

I am personally grateful to these ministers who shared the Sago experience together:

Randy Hughes
Mark Flynn
Jerry Murrell
Wease Day
Mitch Griffin
Ed McDaniels
Frank Spears
Dan and Sue Lowther
Keith and Tuesday Richards
Dennis Estes

I am also deeply grateful to our own Bishop Michael Bransfield and our Chancellor Ellen O'Hara for calling me in the midst of one of the most dismal hours at Sago with their encouragement and prayers of support. Few bishops would take the time to think of doing that, and it was a real spiritual and emotional boost, not only for me, but the other ministers around me who heard the conversation as well.

Chapter 8:
Between a Rock and a Heart Place

During the hours spent at Sago, countless scripture verses were read and recited as soothing oil anointing wounded hearts. It seemed as time went on, however, that four particular portions of scripture came to the forefront over and over again. These four particular scripture passages were used for that very reason as the readings during the Memorial Service held for the miners at the Chapel of West Virginia Wesleyan College in Buckhannon, WV.

The first Bible passage that seemed to strike a chord in our hearts those days were the opening verses of Chapter One of the Gospel of John. One reason they were so poignant is 1:5 which reads: "The light shines on in the darkness, a darkness that did not overcome it." Upon hearing that line, one could not help but consider the utter darkness of a coal mine, the lamps of the miners' hard hats, and the hope that there would be a light leading them out of that deep shaft. John also speaks about the Word of God becoming flesh and dwelling among us and that through this Word all things came to be. Therefore, the world and everything in it, including Sago mine, came into being by the Word of God. It was a horrible notion to think of those miners trapped in an unforgiving black hole. But to consider them as being enfolded in the loving arms of the Word made flesh...to consider the earth around them as the enfleshed Word of God embracing them in love and eternal security…this was a much more positive, freeing, and joyful way of perceiving the situation.

One of the Sago miners had a young son who could be seen throughout the entire long hours of Sago with a Bible under his arm. I don't recall ever seeing him for an instant without that Bible in his hand. And to anyone who would listen to him, he would say: "I would like to read to you my dad's favorite scripture passage." He would then proceed to read Psalm 91, which is all about being rescued from various dangerous situations, and about being sheltered under the wings of a protective God. If one goes to the little church of Lacrima Christi (the Tears of Christ) on the Mount of Olives in Jerusalem, built on the spot where Jesus is said to have wept over Jerusalem, you will notice that the mosaic on the front of the altar there is a depiction of a mother hen sheltering her chicks under her wings. Psalm 91 is a passage of trust and reassurance. The Catholic Church has a song frequently sung at Sunday liturgies based on this section of scripture. It is entitled "On Eagle's Wings" and talks about being raised up on eagle's wings, borne on the breath of God, made to shine like the sun, and being held in the palm of God's hand. When working with Native Americans, I was struck in their artwork that the Holy Spirit is rarely, if ever, shown as a dove. Almost always, the Spirit is portrayed as a red-tailed hawk or a falcon…a bird of strength and courage and swiftness. Psalm 91 gives that sense and gave the people at Sago a great deal of courage, hope and reassurance.

Another commonly recited Scripture passage at Sago was, of course, the 23rd Psalm. Has there ever been a section of Scripture more commonly used in times of trouble throughout the history of the Judeo-Christian tradition? Every word of this Psalm has been reflected upon in Bible commentaries for centuries. Concerning the situation at Sago, it is not much of a stretch to equate the "valley of the shadow of darkness" with the shaft of a coal mine. Someone once made a very astute observation concerning this Psalm. When one finds oneself in the shadow of the valley of darkness; or, in some translations in the shadow of the valley of death, it is important to remember that there can NEVER be a shadow unless there is a LIGHT shining from somewhere. And so to find our way out of that dark valley, we must find the direction the light is coming from in our life and head towards it, just as surely as a coal miner walks toward the light at the mine portal to emerge out of the darkness into sunlight once again. That light for us might be God, Church, the Bible, a priest or minister, a family member or friend, a favorite spot at the lake or mountain. Whatever it is…whatever direction the light is shining from in our life, that is the bearing we must head toward in order to escape the shadowy valley.

The final passage of Scripture that was of enormous importance at Sago was Chapter Eight of Paul's Letter to the Romans: "All things work together for good to those who love God." This was the passage that helped us all to pray for the grace to accept God's will whatever it might prove to be, knowing that all things happened for a reason. We live in absolute surety that God can bring good out of even the most tragic situation. Nobody knows why innocent children get hit by cars and die, or why young mothers die of cancer, or why thousands die in a 911, or why coal miners perish at Sago. So many people spin their spiritual wheels after tragic events searching for ANSWERS. No philosopher, no theologian, no church doctrine has ever given us a completely satisfactory answer as to why good people must suffer and die tragic deaths. The Church does not give us an "answer," but it does give us a PERSON…the person of Jesus Christ to walk with us along our journey of life. It is He who will bear us up and carry us over the rough moments, like the famous "Footprints" prayer reminds us. When you think of it, really, what good would mere answers be anyway? Let's say for a moment that we COULD have an ironclad answer as to why these sufferings and heartaches happen. So what? How does that help us? Does that make us feel even one iota better? No! What we need during such tough times is a PERSON to lean on...not academic answers. It is here that the Church in her wisdom offers us Jesus Christ...the Word made Flesh.

    These then are the four main sections of Sacred Scripture which were read often at Sago and formed the spiritual supports of the roof of God...the wings of refuge over our heads those long hours. In the corner of Sago church late during the night, I at one point noticed a man lying on the floor covered with a blanket. He was fast asleep, but he was mumbling over and over: "I shall fear no evil, for You are with me." If you are going through terrible times in your life right now, I urge you to choose one or all of these scripture passages, to take a line from one of them and repeat it to yourself over and over throughout the day. In doing so, you will find Jesus there carrying you, and a light to lead you home.

Chapter 9: Feathers in the Wind

The nation was ecstatic when the word came that the miners were ALIVE! There has been much speculation as to the chain of events regarding the various messages. Nobody seems to know exactly what message the rescue team radioed out of the mine to the command post. Whether it was "we have found all 12 and they are alive" or "one is alive" we will never know it seems. What we do know is that around midnight many in the command post area were certain they heard that 12 were alive and they went outside, got on their cellphones, and started calling friends and relatives at the church. All of a sudden, several cellphones went off in the church and people were getting the good news. There were also a few people in the church who had radios that could pick up conversations at the command center and mine who thought they had heard the same news. The Sago Baptist Church erupted in celebration. We were all jumping up and down and crying for joy and hugging each other. Even Gov. Manchin was jumping up and down with us.

It was not just that a simple miscommunication took place. The initial announcement was not company-sanctioned and came from the crowds of people. However, after that, there were a whole series of announcements that led people to believe this was really true. I do not know who the men were who made these announcements, but they got up in front of the church and made them from the pulpit microphone. We were told first that the miners were in such good shape that instead of taking them to the hospital in Buckhannon, they were going to bring them down to the church FIRST to see their families. This struck many of us as very strange, knowing that the normal operating procedure in such situations is ALWAYS to take the miners to the hospital first. Yet, another announcement was made a while later saying that two ambulances were being sent up for the miners and they would be down at the church in a few minutes! At that point nearly everyone went outside of the church to be able to greet the miners upon their arrival. This was the only good thing about the series of events that night, for the church had been so tightly packed with people that had the tragic announcement been made with everyone still in there, many people would have been hurt and possibly crushed in the ensuing bedlam.

So there we were outside waiting for the miners. We saw the two ambulances go up the hill. After a long time, one ambulance came down, but instead of turning up to the church, it went straight ahead toward Buckhannon. We all assumed that it must be taking the body of the one dead miner out to the hospital. After that, we waited and waited for what seemed an eternity until the word came that stunned all of us as well as the nation.

I was still outside at that moment. Several people passed out at the news. One elderly lady seemed to either be having a heart attack or going into deep shock. A state trooper fell to his knees sobbing. A fireman collapsed on his back in the mud. We helped to set him up and his eyes were glazed and blank for half an hour before we could communicate with him again. There were many people like that…in such shock that they stared straight ahead with empty eyes for a long time. It was the most heartbreaking moment I have ever experienced.

And may we take a moment here to speak about gossip and spreading false rumors? There is a story that someone once confessed to St. Philip Neri the sin of gossip as if it were of only minor importance. St. Philip Neri, for a penance, told the person to take a feather pillow and go and scatter the feathers in it all over town and then come back to him. When the person returned, St. Philip Neri said, "Now, go and gather up all the feathers back into the pillow." The exasperated person replied that this would be impossible as the wind had blown them far and wide. The saint then made the point on the dangers of the far-reaching effects of gossip and rumors. Can there be any more sublime reminder of this than the false communications at Sago? Let us all consider the next time we feel the urge to spread unverified rumors whether or not we will be able to gather the feathers back up afterwards or not.

Chapter 10: The Beast

You may have had the excitement of riding one of the famous rollercoasters in our nation's various amusement parks: the Steel Phantom, the Loch Ness Monster, or the Beast. But no one has ever had a more devastating rollercoaster ride of emotions than the people of Sago in the early morning hours of January 4th. From the high elation of the midnight pronouncement that all 12 miners were alive, to the message that came nearly 3 hours later which shredded our hearts into confetti and entered our brains like a runaway locomotive.

How does one deal with such pendulum swings of emotion? One noticeable difference between the aftermath of the two announcements was that after the first joyous one, everybody wanted to hug each other. You just HAD to hug someone…everyone. But after the sad announcement, many people wanted to be left alone. Many wandered a space away from whoever they were with, closing themselves up in agony. This is always the action of "The Beast" who seeks invariably to isolate us from God and one another so as to make us easy and helpless targets.

After this came the outpouring of disbelief, sadness, confusion, and grief. The Emotions HAD to come out, for if they had been kept inside, one would become like a cartoon character where a crack slowly spreads out over one's entire façade until he or she crumbles into a million little pieces. People were looking for answers…that so readily available trap. How could this be? Of course, nobody had the answer. We only had questions.

Finally, when it was discovered that people had been aware of the false announcements and had been so long in letting us know the truth, THAT is when the emotions turned to anger and rage. Many said they were going to go and get their guns and would be back fully loaded. Many had rifles or handguns setting in their trucks down at the road and only would have had to walk that far to make good their threats. The ministers responded by asking people to consider that their beloved miners would not want to be remembered that way. Heading off this ominous violent notion was perhaps, in my opinion, the best moment of work that the ministers present at Sago accomplished.

After awhile, the anger dissipated and apologies were heard as people now relied on what had always got them through moments like this: the family bonds of West Virginia. John Denver sang about these hills "whispering" as they call to us. I have not a doubt in my mind that at that moment in Sago, the voices of people's deceased coal miner dads and granddads and great-granddads were whispering on the breeze to be strong, to be tough, to make them proud. Just like the mist ringing our hills on an early mountain morning, the wafts of smoke from the pipes of our ancestors drifted down around us with a reassuring smell of "grandpa" reminding us that the mountains had just taken a few more victims to themselves as the price we pay all too often for living in these emerald hills. It is hard to explain, but never in my life have I felt a sense of "family presence" as was there at 4 am that morning in Sago. They were ALL there with us: every coal miner who ever went into a hole in this state or any other state. Every grandmother who ever lost her husband or son in the mine. Every housewife who had to raise her kids on her own because her husband was killed in a roof cave-in. That dark night in Sago, that dark night of our souls, at that very moment between the darkest night and the first rays of morning, ALL of West Virginia was there with us. And we all KNEW that we HAD to be strong. For our wives, for our sweethearts, for our mothers and grandmothers…for West Virginia…for every coal miner everywhere. And people embraced each other once again, and began walking arm in arm down that muddy road to their trucks, to go home and mourn as generations before them had mourned and many will yet to come. Knowing that after all is said and done, we will put on our hard hats and work belts and we will spit in the gaping hole of those portals and we WILL walk back into those mines and drag that coal out kicking and screaming if we have to. Because no rollercoaster runs without electricity… and there is no electricity without that coal.

Chapter 11: Scars Into Stars

Where do we go from here? After the raw, open wounds of disaster, false rumors, and death are covered over with scars? There are two ways of dealing with scars in life. We can become embarrassed by them and try to cover them up and keep them from everyone's eyes, pretending they aren't there. Or, we can, as Rev. Robert Schuller says, learn to "turn our scars into STARS!"

In 1993 I developed Hodgkins Disease, a cancer of the lymph system. I had 3 surgeries, removal of my spleen, and 41 radiation treatments. My hair fell out, my salivary glands were affected and I had to use artificial saliva, I developed a bed sore which took months to heal, my stitches rejected and seeped for nearly 10 years afterward. In 2004 a heart attack resulted in a quadruple heart bypass operation, two carotid artery surgeries, a paralyzed right vocal chord, and a damaged femoral nerve in my leg. I have scars on my body literally from head to toe. Turning scars into stars is something I have had to learn the hard way.

Whenever we are in the midst of a dark night in our life, one of the most important things to do is to look UP. In the famous Fellini film "La Dolce Vita" there is a scene in which a helicopter is flying over the city of Rome with a huge cross it is hauling suspended beneath it, and nobody looks UP to see it. There is a reason why our Savior Jesus Christ died high on a cross. So that we would have to LOOK UP from the depths of our despair in order to see our salvation. The Bible reminds us to "look up to the mountains from whence comes our help." If it were not for the dark of night times in life, we would be unable to see the stars! In every night, no matter how deep, there are glimmers of faith to guide us as surely as the constellations guide sailors over rough waters. The first step in turning scars into stars is LOOKING UP to see them.

If all we ever had in life was sunshine, we would end up in a very dry desert. We need the thunderstorm moments of life to make new growth spring up. The terrible thunderstorm that took place the morning of the disaster in Sago is one that people will never forget. But to wallow in the mud of that storm would be to go against all that those miners believed in. Instead we search for the place in our lives where those torrents of water have nourished new life. What new values, new lessons, new faith, new relationships, new reconciliations that have been dammed up in our hearts for so long have those waters caused to open up. What waters has the storm of Sago caused to gush forth from our hearts? For many, Sago will be a true Noah experience, as they allow God's hands to be their ark carrying them over these rough waters to a place of safety and new life. For many people, the Sago mine that swallowed our miners is the whale that swallowed Jonah…and our hearts as well. It was when Jonah agreed to hear and obey God's word that the whale spewed him forth back onto dry land. If we are feeling swallowed up by the Sago whale, one way back to dry land is listening to God's word and following it.

Sago, in the end, can be a grave of death, or a tomb of resurrection. As we approach the memory of those days in our hearts and minds, we approach as did Mary Magdalene on Easter morning, expecting to weep at the tomb of death. But if we listen to God speaking to us, if we can change our scars into stars, then, like Mary we will see angels at the place where the dead body was laid. And those angels will say to us: "Why do you look for the living among the dead? He is not here, He is Risen." In other words, LOOK UP! And then, along with Mary Magdalene, we will turn around and catch sight of Jesus standing there. He may seem to be in the guise of the gardener, or our brother or sister, or our mailman or grocery store clerk, or our minister or priest. But if we LOOK UP and TURN AROUND, we will find our scars turning into stars. For we are dust, and to dust we shall return. BUT, the dust we shall return to is STARDUST!

Chapter 12:
The Hatfields and the McCloys

In the aftermath of almost any disaster or tragedy, a common emotional response is a desire to determine who, if anyone, is responsible, and to affix blame. There are often a variety of motivations, both positive and negative, behind this tendency: anger, hurt, legal options, a desire for revenge, intense grief, concern for the safety of miners in the future. One or all of these factors may be the driving force in the finger-pointing that follows most such events...whether it be Hurricane Katrina or the Sago Mine disaster.

The one historical event that most outsiders are familiar with in the annals of West Virginia is, of course, the famous family feud between the Hatfields of WestVirginia and the McCoys of Kentucky. That feud took place at a time following the War Between the States when the boundary between these two states was still very iffy. The families had fought on different sides during the war. Despite the famous account of the feud beginning over a pig, its roots were much deeper than that, having a lot more to do with competition over political, legal, and economic opportunities and positions than any concern over who was hosting the next pork barbecue.

The roots of the long and ongoing relationship between West Virginia coal miners and the coal companies that employ them are just as deep, and it would be a most superficial perspective to analyze them solely on the basis of a lightning strike or ruptured seals. Coal miners and coal companies have been both family and adversaries throughout our history. At one point in our past the U.S. government actually sent troops in to settle a strike in our state, and I believe that during those coal wars, West Virginia is the only state in which the federal government used airplanes to bomb its own citizens! The movie "Matewan" graphically portrays the struggle for unionization in our coal fields.

And yet, to think of miners and the companies solely in adversarial terms would be inaccurate, for they each depend on the other for survival. To understand the dynamics of coal mining, we must once again turn to family. The struggles, the arguments, the injustices, the finger-pointing that takes place between miners and the companies can perhaps best be understood in the sense of a family feud. Miners and the companies are family in that one cannot exist without the other. Sometimes arguments come to blows and sometimes people die on both sides, but in the end it remains family.

In the case of Sago, if we think of Ben Hatfield as a coal company representative, and of Randy McCloy as symbolic of coal miners in general, what can we learn from each? The media and many others, in the frantic finger-pointing following Sago, targeted Mr. Hatfield to a large extent for the manner in which the announcements were made at Sago Church. In my opinion, this is very unfair and unfortunate. There is no family in our entire state whose surname is more synonymous with West Virginia than "Hatfield." Someone like Ben Hatfield IS West Virginia. Being intentionally secretive or hurtful to the Sago families would have been the furthest thing from his mind. On the contrary, his stated desire several times during those days was to offer accurate and truthful information in as timely a manner as possible. Most people at Sago Baptist Church during those nerve-wracking hours looked forward to announcements by Mr. Hatfield, for of all the spokespersons who did them, he was by far the most sincere, personal, and caring. I believe that the miscommunications in those awful early morning hours were less a result of any intentional cover-up by this man, and more due to the eagerness of people for good news, the ready availability of cellphones and radios, and the lack of patience to wait for an accurate report. It is always easiest to single out one person to blame in situations like this, but in this particular case it was more like a Domino effect in which many people were involved in passing on erroneous information…for the most part unintentionally. And unless I am mistaken, the miners who died in the Logan Co. mine fire disaster just a short time after Sago were relatives of Mr. Hatfield. So he knows firsthand the pain of losing loved ones in the mines.

Yet, we cannot forget the McCloys of the world. Just as the "Hatfield" name symbolizes West Virginia, so does "McCloy" now stand for every Coal Miner in this state's history. The famous mountains of our state are not simply geographic features. They represent the courageous, hard-working BACKBONES of the coal miners who made this state what it is today. Randy McCloy stands in ALL of their shoes and HIS name will now and forever be a symbol of West Virginia as much as is "Hatfield."

Here is a young miner who went into a dangerous occupation in order to provide a good life for his family. A young man with many dreams and plans. Coal companies and the government OWE IT to brave men like this to make the mines as safe as possible and to put safety FIRST before production or profits. Coal companies in general are notorious for taking the least expensive route in mine safety and equipment. Yet, the dollars spent on survival stations, proper equipment and training more than pay for themselves, for nothing is ever as costly as having to close a mine down after a disaster. The resulting loss in production and revenue far outweighs even the most expensive safety system.

One of the problems during the famous Hatfield-

McCoy Feud was biased county courts, judges, and political favoritism. The same thing occurs in the relationship between coal companies, government agencies, and miners. MSHA is sorely lacking today in truly experienced mine inspectors, and there are numerous stories of inspectors giving a passing mark only to be followed within hours by rock falls or other mishaps. One of the problems nowadays is that trainings, whether for inspectors or miners, are too often politically based and led and conducted by bureaucrats with little or no actual mining experience. Such trainings ought to be conducted by the most experienced mine foreman available in the state, and not only miners, but company officials and government officials ought to attend regularly.

If there is any way to seek a solution to the often bitter and disappointing relationship between coal mining companies and coal miners, it must I think be found to some degree in the way that Jesus interacted, on behalf of the poor, with the authorities of his time. Over and over again, we see Jesus dealing with social injustices, money-hungry tax collectors, nepotism, and unfair labor relations with the same basic approach: truthful assessments, honest perspectives, bluntness in presenting the issues, the necessity of adequate reparation when injustices have taken place, AND a willingness to forgive those who have the courage to change and accept such principles. We see it, for example, in the stories of Matthew and Zaccheus, in the parables of the laborers in the vineyard, and in the story of the unjust steward. The same concepts can be found in the stories of Hebrew slavery in Egypt, the conversations between Moses and Pharoah, the entreaties made by Jeremiah to the authorities of his age, the scales of justice in the lives of David and Solomon, and so forth.

Translating the example and method of Jesus to the arbitration tables of coal companies and unions, we see that after a disaster like Sago, the need is likewise for a truthful and honest assessment of what happened, an honest perspective on why it happened, a bluntness in presenting the issues in government hearings and not politicizing them, the necessity of adequate reparation for the victims' families, and a willingness to forgive as people jointly work toward making the coal mine a safer place to work.

One other point. There were many times in which Jesus confronted unjust officials or businessmen openly in the midst of many witnesses in public places. But very often, Jesus follows that up with a more private, personal contact such as dinner in the person's home. We see this in the cases of Matthew and Zaccheus. Historically speaking, coal company representatives (the so-called "supers") lived in the big houses on the hill, while the miners lived in the squalor of the company homes. West Virginia has had the sad experience that many of the coal, gas, oil, and timber businesses which come here for our natural resources are often companies with out-of-state owners who have very little notion of this state or its people. This only serves to further polarize an already flammable relationship between the companies and employees. Something that would go a long way toward greater understanding would be for company owners and officials to have a local presence. Besides the penthouse in Manhattan, a white clapboard house near the hollers visited a few times a year would help to create some mutual respect. If an owner insists on a brick house with columns on top of the hill, so be it. But come and walk the streets of Sago, or Logan or Williamson or Lumberport or Philippi and meet the employees who go down in those holes. Get to know them by their first names. Meet their wives and children and grandparents. Come and see what makes the people here tick. We don't care if you wear coveralls and mud-kickers, or if you insist on walking around in a three-piece suit. But come and be here once in awhile. Breathe this mountain air and see the smiles on our children's faces. Do THAT, and there will never be another argument between coal company management and employees on the absolute utter necessity of top-notch mine safety and survival programs and equipment.

Chapter 13: State of the Union

A word on unions, which nowadays seem to be anything BUT what the word implies. My grandparents had two pictures on their living room wall. One was of Franklin Delano Roosevelt. The other was of John L. Lewis. There was a time when miners credited those two men with their very survival. The unions had a solidarity which served to greatly enhance the working conditions of miners. My hometown was a UMWA stronghold and all the miners then were union. Over the past three decades, the unions have basically shot themselves in the foot. Back in the 1970s there were strikes every time management turned around. Strikes if the soap supply for the wash house was late coming in. Strikes became so commonplace over such trivial matters that companies were almost forced to strike back. Today the unions are nothing at all like they used to be and many consider them more a hindrance than a help. If I am not mistaken, Sago is not a union mine. Neither was Quecreek. Many mines today are not. Union politics, the Yablonski murder, the rise in automated mining, alternative sources of energy, and greater unemployment in the industry all served to shatter the solidarity of the union.

Everyone knew that our late Holy Father, Pope John Paul II, was a firm supporter of unions. What would the Solidarity movement in Poland have been without his support and encouragement? The Catholic Church has supported the labor movement around the world for over a century. Unions are important. If there is one thing the UMWA can be proud of, it was the way in which it provided medical and health care for its members and their families over the years, especially for the widows of coal miners. The Bible repeatedly exhorts us to be sure to care of widows, and few have done as good a job historically as the UMWA. Many miners and retired miners today, however, claim that recent practices leave a lot to be desired in this regard.

Solidarity against unfair labor practices, vigilance against unsafe conditions, and care and concern for miners and their families, must always be the hallmark of any union. Too often today, those elected to union positions forget where they came from. Once elected, they too often turn up their noses to the membership and use their positions to hobnob with the management and government officials to further their own personal agendas. Miners resent having to pay dues to belong to such organizations. Would the Sago mine have been safer had it been a union mine? Would the relationship between the company and the miners have been better or worse? Would the families of the Sago miners be better off or not? Those questions cannot be answered.

We do know that there WAS a UNION at Sago, whether UMWA or not. That union existed in the brotherhood of the men of that shift who worked together in SOLIDARITY day after day. Just as the 12 disciples huddled together in the upper room awaiting the coming of the Holy Spirit upon them, those 12 Sago miners huddled together in their lower room awaiting their moment with God. In the end, the greatest union of all time is the union between God and humanity, the union between heaven and earth, and the union between us and those who have gone before us marked with the sign of faith. The Catholic Church has always preached the SOLIDARITY that exists among the Church Triumphant (in heaven), the Church Suffering (in Purgatory), and the Church Militant (on earth). There is but a thin veil between this world and the next. Nothing UNITES people more than mutual prayer. Nothing creates greater SOLIDARITY than suffering together. Nothing leads to greater activism and SOCIAL JUSTICE than mutual compassion in the midst of life's tragedies. We hear the voices and prayers of those who have gone before us calling us to act with justice and compassion.

    It is here that our churches must take the lead. In the Catholic Church we celebrate a Red Mass every year for people in the legal profession. Many hold a Blue Mass for those in law-enforcement. What if we celebrated a Mass and/or nondenominational service every year on behalf of all those involved in the coal industry? A time of prayer in which company officials, union representatives, MSHA inspectors, legislators, miners and their families could all come together and pray for greater solidarity and safety. What if besides a March for Life every January, we had a March of Mine Safety once a year as well? What would it be like to see 100,000 coal miners marching down Constitution Ave. and meeting with their Congressional representatives to discuss mine safety legislation? What if we encouraged mine foremen to go to work an hour early every day and stay an hour later, and during that time meet INDIVIDUALLY with every miner to go over safety procedures, and continue that process until every miner on the payroll had been seen, and after which to start from the beginning all over again? My father did that when he was general mine foreman of two mines and had the best safety record of any mine in the area. There are chaplains for fire departments, for law enforcement, for hospitals, prisons, hospices. What if we priests and ministers began to offer ourselves as chaplains for the mines? What if every mine had its own chaplain? How might that further goodwill among miners and between miners and company officials? Couldn't the state help create such a chaplaincy program and tie it in with the faith-based initiative program already in existence? What if we offered our church halls and retreat centers free of charge for mine safety conferences and workshops?

It is unfair to point fingers at coal companies or unions when we, as church communities, could be doing SO MUCH MORE to promote social justice and reconciliation. The Pastoral Letter of the Appalachian Bishops a few years ago reminded us that we are all connected in the web of life and responsible to one another. In today's day and age of economic upheaval, downsizing, and outsourcing, ALL West Virginians, including churches, must come together in mutual understanding and support in the spheres of industry and the economy. Perhaps the greatest legacy of Sago would be if it were to be seen as a catalyst for a general coming together of industry, government, labor, and religion in a mutual attempt to improve safety, communications, and training. As St. Francis said, "Let us begin, for as of yet we have done nothing."

Chapter 14:
We're Not in Kansas Anymore, Toto

After days of hoping against hope and the tremendous emotional strain of the good news followed by the announcement that the miners were dead, and the pain of the loss the families experienced, you would think that the very least to expect was that they would be able to bury their loved ones in peace. This was not to be the case with the families of the Sago miners. Something occurred so unexpected and unbelievable as to leave us stunned and heartsick. Members of a sect in Kansas decided to come to West Virginia and picket the miners' funerals. Their basic premise was that America is going to the dogs and has become a heathen nation. Somehow, in their minds, they believed the Sago miners and families symbolized this national demise. More commonly picketing the funerals of men and women in the armed forces, this group decided to use the pain and heartache of the miners' families for their own publicity purposes. The utter callousness of this action left the entire state of West Virginia nearly speechless over how anyone could possibly pile additional pain and stress upon families that were already going through the worst kind of sadness.

Members of this Kansas group came to Buckhannon and Philippi and attempted to make good their threats. While attending some of the miners' funerals in Buckhannon, the group could be seen trying to picket, but the police kept them at enough of a distance so as not to disturb the mourners at the funeral homes. The protesters were also kept at a distance during the memorial service that was held at the chapel of WV Wesleyan College. The excellent work of the law-enforcement community probably benefited the Kansas group the most, for had they been permitted to get close to the funerals and chapels, violence most certainly would have erupted, for the people of West Virginia would have no patience for that kind of behavior.

Yet the Kansas protesters unwittingly served to highlight all that is best with the culture of West Virginia, for nothing throughout the entire Sago story more revealed the sense of FAMILY that exists here. Miners from MacDowell and Logan Counties in the southern part of the state came up to stand guard at some of the funerals and make sure the families would not be disturbed. Everyone was on the lookout for Kansas license plates, and the police were notified immediately if any were seen entering the state. Here in Philippi, where everyone knows each other, people were quick to notice unfamiliar faces hanging around the perimeter of the courtyard square the night the candlelight service was held, and made sure they stayed on the perimeter and were not able to get close enough to make a disturbance. The law enforcement community was present at every funeral home and church service involving the miners and saw to it that people could pay their last respects to the miners in peace.

It was fitting that scarcely a week or two after all the miner funerals were over, we had a service at our local funeral home for a young woman who had died unexpectedly of an aneurism. She was originally from Kansas and much of her family had come out from Kansas to be at her funeral. They expressed their embarrassment and apologies that anyone from their state would have tried to hurt the miners' families as the Kansas group attempted. These people from Kansas were true-blue, hard-working, typical down-home American families who thought and felt pretty much the same way that all of us in West Virginia do. The people here welcomed and embraced them and showed them all the hospitality for which our state is so famous. And it was a good lesson in not judging an entire state by only a few of its inhabitants…something which the national media often does in regard to West Virginia.

The Kansas protesters were treated like the Wicked Witch of the West and melted away into oblivion having accomplished nothing with their shock tactics. The second Kansas group, who had come to mourn one of their own loved ones, reminded all of us of the lesson Dorothy learned in the movie: "There's no place like home." Take us home, country roads!

Chapter 15:
Sweet Home Alabama

As long as we are discussing visitors from other states and their impact on the Sago event and aftermath, we would be remiss not to mention the wonderful families of Brookwood, Alabama who, out of their own expenses, came up to West Virginia to be with the families of the Sago miners. Brookwood was the site of the mine disaster that took place on September 23, 2001 in which many more miners died than at Sago. But Brookwood took place less than two weeks after 9-11 and did not get nearly the national publicity as did Sago.

Unlike the people from Kansas who came here to add salt to the wounds of already hurting families, the people from Alabama came here to dress and soothe the emotional wounds of Sago. There were four families that came here from Alabama, all of which had lost loved ones in the Brookwood disaster. Those miners' bodies were not recovered for over a month and their families had to wait for weeks before they knew the outcome. They are still dealing with the coal company, MSHA, and the state and federal governments and many, to this date, have not received a cent in reparation to help them.

These Alabama families came here and began meeting with the families of the Sago miners. They had such a beautiful and caring way about them, as they knew firsthand what the hurt and despair felt like. They attended many of the miners' funerals and also the memorial services that were held at

Alderson-Broaddus College in Philippi and at Wesleyan College in Buckhannon. They met with many of us ministers and there were several lunches involving ministers, the Alabama families, and Sago family members. The Alabama families shared their experiences with the Sago ones. They explained what to expect with the emotional and grieving processes, what to expect from the coal company, MSHA, the government, the legal and political processes, and they gave the Sago families a great deal of good advice on what to watch out for in the way of scams from those who would seek to profit from their misfortune. This one-on-one friendly "kitchen counseling" was undoubtedly better than any other attempt at "grief counseling" in those days immediately following the disaster. Many of the Alabama folk stayed here in West Virginia for nearly two weeks afterward helping the Sago families. They continue to be in touch by mail, email, and phone and have provided an important network of support. It almost begs one to ask the question: "Shouldn't there be a national or even international support group for the families of those who are killed in the coal mines that is of, by and for those families?"

As a minister, I will never again read the words of Jesus in the gospel to "love your neighbor as yourself" without thinking of Alabama. No one has ever brought those words to life better than the caring people of Brookwood. Without a doubt, a bond has been forged between the Sago families, the people of Buckhannon and of Philippi, and those families from Brookwood, Alabama…a bond that will never be broken. In a deep and personal way, our two states have bonded and become kindred spirits. I don't think that anything could break that bond unless it were a Mountaineer/Crimson Tide matchup in a major bowl game! Even then, our competition would be congenial and familial, for Sago, Buckhannon, Philippi, and Brookwood have become FAMILY forever. All of us here extend our special thanks and prayers to the

Brookdale families that gave of their own time and expense, and for whom Sago brought back many memories of their own. Please let us all remember them and keep them in our prayers:
1) Donna Boyd of Brookwood
2) Ricky Rose of Cottondale
3) Janice "Cookie" Nail of Dora
4) David and Wanda Blevins of Tuscaloosa

There was a sign in Buckhannon after Sago which read: "Heaven has 12 new angels." Heaven may have 12 new angels, but these four families from Alabama have become West Virginia's special "Dixie Angels" and we will never forget them. They always have a place in our hearts and in our homes and we hope they return to us often.

Chapter 16: Saved by Sago

I am a Catholic priest. I was ordained to the priesthood on June 6, 1987 and have spent my entire priestly life in West Virginia. At the time of my ordination, it could not be said that I had a personal relationship with Jesus Christ. Oh, I had attended church all my life. Growing up, my hometown was 90% Catholic…a population of 4000 with SIX Catholic churches. There was the Polish church, the Slovak church, the Hungarian church, the Irish church, the Italian church, and the Greek church. And a Russian Orthodox church for good measure. I accepted all the precepts of the Catholic Church and still do. We lived just across the street from St. Anthony's, the Italian church in our neighborhood of Little Italy. As a child, I could practically roll out of bed and into church. When our new church was built, I could look out the bedroom window on a Sunday morning and see through the glass doors of the church how far along in the Mass the priest was and thereby know how much time I had to get ready for the next one. There were four Masses at our parish every Sunday morning.

Besides Sunday Mass, it was taken for granted that one would also attend the various devotions such as 40 Hours, Novenas, and Stations of the Cross, not to mention weekly Confession. Our "Sunday school" was Saturday mornings from 9 until Noon, followed always by Confession. Those were the Baltimore Catechism days. The Sister of St. Joseph from Baden, PA would give us a question from the Catechism and a certain amount of minutes to memorize the answer. When the time was up, we had to stand up one by one and recite the answer. If we did all our answers correctly, we got a holy card of St. Anthony or St. Francis or Mary or some other saint. If we got the answers wrong, we missed recess and had to sweep the church basement. So by the time we had received our Confirmation, we knew that Baltimore Catechism backwards and forwards.

I remember the shock that went through the Catholic world when the Second Vatican Council took place in the early 1960s. Previous to that, Mass was in Latin, the priest had his back to the people, there was only one New Testament reading, no responsorial psalm, and the Gospel was always Matthew. There was no Sign of Peace, no Communion in the hand. In fact, most people rarely went to Communion at all other than at Christmas and Easter. John's Gospel was read after Communion.

And then came Vatican II, with Mass in English, the priest facing the people, more readings and psalms, lessons from all the Gospels, a Sign of Peace, Communion in the hand, and most of all: questions, questions, questions. You see, the Baltimore Catechism had taught us all the ANSWERS. BUT WE NEVER HAD UNDERSTOOD THE QUESTIONS!!! We never knew where the questions came from, why they existed, what they were to accomplish, why they were important.

The Church was suddenly alive and QUESTIONING. Everyone was searching...not for answers but for questions. New questions. This quest...this journey...led many of us to consider priestly vocations. We wanted to know all we could about God...about Jesus...about the Bible...about the Church and the Mass and the Sacraments. And so I finally became a priest, and at the moment of my ordination in 1987, I knew a lot ABOUT Jesus. But I did not know JESUS personally.

That came in 1993 when I struggled with cancer and barely survived. It was during that ordeal that I realized questions and answers BOTH meant very little in such times. What a person REALLY needs then is a PERSON to walk with and talk with and lean on. It was at that time that Jesus became a personal friend, confidante, companion, shoulder to lean on, hope and joy in my life.

But my dear friends, the events of Sago made me realize that it is not enough to know the answers. It is not enough to know the questions. It is not enough to accept Jesus as a friend and personal companion. There is a big difference between accepting Jesus as a FRIEND and accepting Jesus as LORD and SAVIOR. In the emotional turmoil of Sago...in the desperation of heart...in the profound praying...THIS was the main lesson. For how can you pray for miners to be SAVED unless there is a SAVIOR to hear you? As mentioned earlier in this book, people at Sago bonded almost instantly. Friendships sprung up. People felt like family. But bonding and friendship and family feelings were not enough. We were all reaching for something more. For when you pray from way down deep in your heart for miners to be saved...you can't help but sooner or later realizing that you are praying for yourself to be saved with them. When you beseech Jesus as Savior on behalf of others, Jesus is quick to say, "And what about YOU my son...my daughter?"

As we stood there for 3 days in Sago Baptist Church...that little church became Jacob's Well. It became the Pool of Siloam. It became Mount Tabor. It became the Garden of Gethsemane. It became the Tomb of Lazarus. And it became, most of all, Calvary, where one could not but echo the words of the Roman centurion: "Truly this man is the Son of God." Person after person at Sago asked to "be saved." Young and old alike. And after Sago, so many hundreds of people attending churches for the first time were asking to be saved. I witnessed this and saw the glow in their faces afterwards.

And then our Barbour County Ministerial Association held a nondenominational Memorial Service for the miners at Wilcox Chapel of Alderson-Broaddus College on January 10th. The service of light was moving; not only was it moving, but it made me question how much darkness I still had in my soul. The readings from Scripture were profound. The sermon by Rev. Destry Daniels of the Methodist Belington Circuit moved me in a way I cannot find words to express. The task of doing the final benediction was left to me. By that point, after the spiritual intensity of Sago, after the example of so many who had sought Jesus as their Savior, after the realization over those three days of how much I still fell short of accepting Jesus totally, after the respect I felt for some of the ministers in attendance that night who had been with me at Sago and who were such examples of accepting Jesus....all of those emotions hit me at that moment as I approached the podium, and there was such a burning need in my heart to be closer to Jesus. Not just as a friend, but to accept Him as the power and authority over my life and to accept the gift of salvation of which I had always felt so unworthy and undeserving.

My childhood and Vatican II and priesthood and the Sago experience all bubbled up from depths inside me that I did not even know were there, and I knew that I had to make a greater commitment to Christ right then and there. So as we ministers had planned, we invited people after the service to come and talk and pray with us if they felt the need, and we encouraged, in a very low-key manner, for anyone who had not yet accepted Jesus as their Lord and Savior to come and be saved. And then I invited Rev. Randy Hughes (who wrote the Forward to this book) whom I had met at Sago for the first time, and Rev. Dean Davidson of

Philippi Baptist Church, and Rev. Bob Wilkins of Heart and Hand Ministries, both of whom have made me feel so much at home in Philippi, to come forward and join me. And I asked them if they would please pray with me and help me to accept Jesus as my Savior too. From now on, I shall mark my life as before and after January 10, 2006, for I cannot find words to tell you what a weight and burden felt lifted from my shoulders that night.

I close this book with the passage from Paul's Letter to the Romans (Chapter 10, verses 9,10 and 13) which Revs. Hughes, Davidson and Wilkins had me pray together with them. And I encourage you, my dear reader, if you have not yet accepted Jesus Christ as your Savior, to pray this prayer with us and with all of Sago, and to then as soon as possible go to your pastor and pray it together with him or her, so that we may continue this pilgrim journey of ours in this life as true brothers and sisters in the Lord, until that day when we are reunited with our beloved miners and see that they too have been SAVED BY SAGO all along.

Dear Jesus, I believe that You are the Son of God.
I believe that You shed Your Precious Blood
for the remission of sins.
Please forgive me of my sins and come into my heart.
Thank you for saving me.
Amen.

Additional copies may be purchased from:

McClain Printing Company
P.O. Box 403
212 Main Street
Parsons, WV 26287
1-800-654-7179
FAX: 304-478-4658
E-mail: mcclain@mcclainprinting.com
Website: www.mcclainprinting.com
Visa, MasterCard, Discover and American Express accepted.